The Sikh Wedding

The Sikh Wedding

Text by Mohinder Singh

Photographs by Sondeep Shankar

UBS Publishers' Distributors Pvt. Ltd.

IN ASSOCIATION WITH

National Institute of Panjab Studies

NATIONAL INSTITUTE OF PANJAB STUDIES, NEW DELHI

Advisory Committee:

Prof. Mulk Raj Anand
Prof. Amrik Singh
Prof. Bipan Chandra
Dr. J.S. Neki
Prof. B.N. Goswamy

Series Editor: Dr. Mohinder Singh

UBS Publishers' Distributors Pvt. Ltd.

5 Ansari Road, **New Delhi-110 002**
Phones: 011-23273601-04, 23266646 ● Fax: 23276593, 23274261
E-mail: ubspd@ubspd.com

10 First Main Road, Gandhi Nagar, **Bangalore-560 009**
Phones: 080-2253903, 2263901, 2263902 ● Fax: 2263904
E-mail: ubspdbng@eth.net

8/1-B, Chowringhee Lane, **Kolkata-700 016**
Phones: 033-22521821, 22522910, 22529473 ● Fax: 22523027
E-mail: ubspdcal@cal.vsnl.net.in

60, Nelson Manickam, Aminjikarai, **Chennai-600 029**
Phones: 044-23746222, 23746351-2 ● Fax: 23746287
E-mail: ubspd@che.ubspd.com

5 A, Rajendra Nagar, **Patna-800 016**
Phones: 0612-2672856, 2673973, 2686170 ● Fax: 2686169
E-mail: ubspdpat1@sancharnet.in

143 M P Nagar, Zone I, **Bhopal-462 011**
Phones: 0755-5203183, 5203193, 2555228 ● Fax: 2555285
E-mail: ubspdbhp@sancharnet.in

No. 40/7940, Convent Road, **Ernakulam-682 035**
Phones: 0484-2353901, 2363905 ● Fax: 2365511
E-mail: ubspdchn@eth.net

2nd floor Apeejay Chambers, 5 Wallace Street, Fort, **Mumbai-400 001**
Phones: 56376922, 56376923 ● Fax: 56376921
E-mail: ubspdmum@mum.ubspd.com

1st floor, Halvasiya Court Annexe, 11-MG Marg, Hazratganj, **Lucknow-226 001**

Visit us at www.ubspd.com & www.gobookshopping.com

© National Institute of Panjab Studies

First Published 2004

Cover & Book Design: Dushyant Parasher

Processed and Printed by
International Print-O-Pac Ltd., Delhi

Cover: A groom seated on a specially decorated mare on way to the bride's house

Half title page: A couple circumambulating the Guru Granth Sahib

Title spread: Vatna *being applied to the groom*

Foreword

The National Institute of Panjab Studies was established in 1990 to promote research on different aspects of Punjabi life and letters. The Panjab University, Chandigarh, subsequently recognized the Institute as an advanced centre of learning. Apart from promoting research, the Institute has also been organising lectures, seminars and conferences. Some conferences were also organized in collaboration with other institutions such as the Department of Multicultural Education, University of London, Department of South Asian Studies, University of Michigan, Ann Arbor and the Centre for Global Studies, University of California, Santa Barbara. To mark fifty years of India's independence the Institute organised an international seminar on 'Partition in Retrospect' in collaboration with the India International Centre, New Delhi.

In connection with the tercentenary of the Khalsa in 1999, the Institute took up a major research project of locating and cataloguing relics belonging to the Sikh Gurus and other historical personalities. Our research team led by the Director of the Institute, visited various parts of India and Pakistan, and located and listed a number of valuable relics. During their fieldwork, our team located some very precious relics such as the *chola* of Guru Nanak, the *chola* of Guru Hargobind, *chola, dastar* and other relics of Guru Gobind Singh and Mata Sahib Kaur, sword-belt, *godri* and flag of Maharaja Ranjit Singh. Our team took pictures of these and other precious relics and recorded popular history connected with these objects. As a result of the initiative taken by the Institute, INTACH has taken up the conservation of some of these relics.

With a view to sharing the results of our research with the larger audience and creating awareness for proper preservation of the endangered heritage of Panjab and conservation of the valuable relics, the Institute decided to bring out a series of pictorial books under the Panjab Heritage Series.

Four books published in the first phase were launched in the Rashtrapati Bhawan on the birthday of Guru Nanak Dev in November, 2001. In view of the encouraging response the Institute is now preparing another set of four books in the second phase.

The Institute would like to record its gratitude to the Department of Culture, Government of India, for its initial grant for preparing a 'Catalogue of the Sikh Relics', to the Government of the National Capital of Delhi for its financial support for publication of these books and to various institutions and individuals for allowing the Institute's team access to their rich collections. I would also like to thank my colleagues on the Governing Council and staff of the Institute, without whose active cooperation it would not have been possible to bring out these volumes.

Manmohan Singh

President
National Institute of Panjab Studies
Bhai Vir Singh Marg
New Delhi - 110 001

Acknowledgements

The National Institute of Panjab Studies acknowledges its gratitude to the following for their contribution to the Panjab Heritage Series:

- The National Museum, New Delhi
- The National Archives of India, New Delhi
- The Panjab State Archives and the Panjab State Museum, Chandigarh, Patiala and Amritsar
- The Shiromani Gurdwara Prabandhak Committee, Amritsar, for permitting us to take photographs of the relics in the Toshakhana of the Golden Temple and sacred weapons at the Akal Takhat, Amritsar, Takhat Sri Kesgarh Sahib, Anandpur, Takhat Damdama Sahib, Talwandi Sabo
- Takhat Sri Patna Sahib, Bihar
- Takhat Sri Hazoor Sahib, Nanded
- The Sikh Regimental Centre, Ramgarh
- Capt. Amarinder Singh, New Moti Bagh Palace, Patiala
- The Bagrian family at Quila Bagrian
- The Sangha family of Drolli Bhai Ki
- Family of Mai Desan, Chak Fateh Singhwala
- Family of Bhai Rupa, Village Bhai Rupa, Dist. Bhatinda
- Family of Bhai Dalla, Talwandi Sabo, Dist. Bhatinda
- Mrs. Jyoti Rai, American Numismatic Society
- Dr. Jean Marie Lafont, French Embassy, New Delhi
- Gurdwara Sri Hemkunt Sahib Management Trust, Kanpur
- S. Bhajan Singh, Chairman, Singapore Sikh Education Foundation
- Department of Archaeology and Museums, Government of Pakistan, for permission to take photographs of relics of Maharaja Ranjit Singh and his family in Princess Bamba collection, Lahore Fort Museum, Lahore
- Punjab and Sind Bank, for the paintings used from their collection
- Hardev Singh, Raghu Rai, Ashok Dilwali, Gurmeet Thukral, Manohar Singh, Satpal Danish and Dushyant Parasher for allowing to use their pictures
- Dr S S Bhugra, Dr Susan Stronge, J D Dewan, Mrs Mohinder Singh, Ranjit Kaur and Ashwani Kumar for their input to the project
- Faqir Syed Saif-ud-Din, Fakir Khana Museum, Lahore
- Syed Afzal Haidar, Advocate, Supreme Court, Pakistan
- The Victoria & Albert Museum, London.

Facing page: Bride being escorted to the venue of Anand Karaj

Double spread on pages 8-9: Sehrabandi ceremony being performed by sisters

Double spread on pages 10-11: Women of the groom's family selecting bangles

Double spread on pages 12-13: The bride, her sisters and friends during the mehndi ceremony

Double spread on pages 14-15: People dance their way to the marriage venue

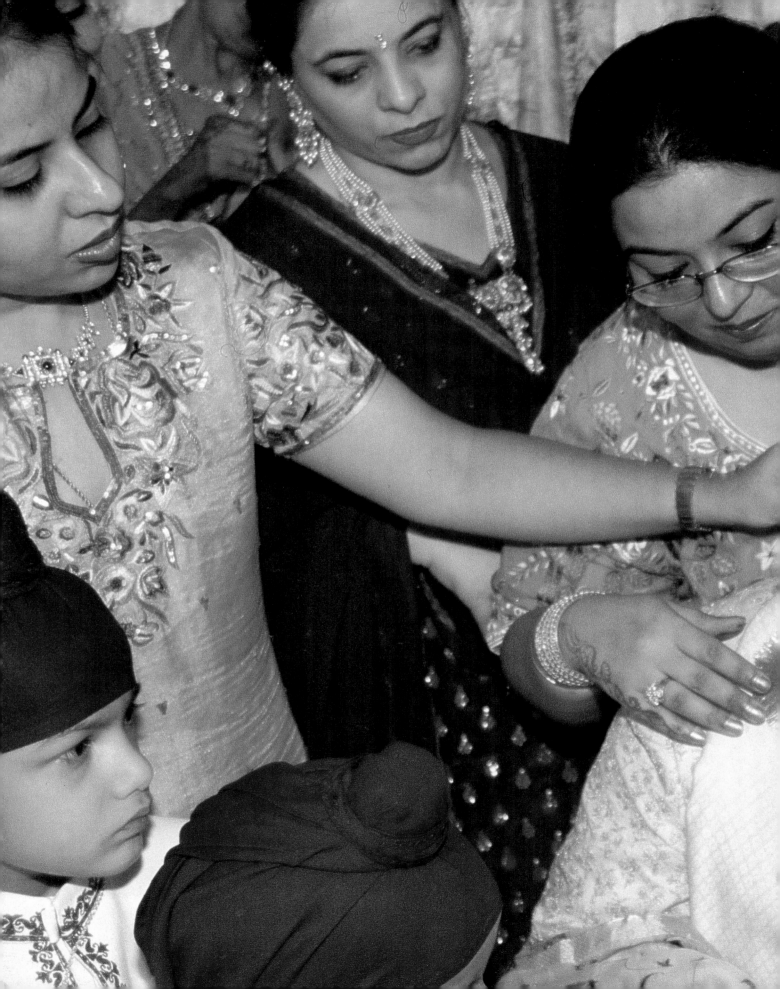

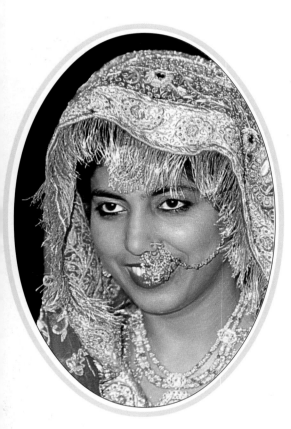

Above: A Sikh bride

Facing page: A newly wed Sikh couple

While the Sikhs follow several popular pre- and post-Panjabi marriage customs their marriage rites are performed through *Anand Karaj*. Several Sikh scholars trace the origin of *Anand Karaj* ceremony to the days of the third Guru, Amar Das. According to information supplied by the supporters of the Anand Marriage Bill, which was passed in the Imperial Legislative Council of India in 1909, the fourth Guru, Ram Das devised a distinct marriage ceremony for the Sikhs, popularly known as *Anand Karaj*. According to Sikh tradition, a Sikh named Randhawa petitioned Guru Amar Das to the effect that the village priest had refused to solemnize his daughter's marriage because he and his family members had embraced Sikhism. Thereupon the Guru asked Ram Das, his son-in-law and successor, to solemnize the marriage of Randhawa's daughter according to Sikh rituals. It was for this purpose that the fourth Guru composed the hymns called *lavaan*, which were subsequently included in *Guru Granth Sahib* by the fifth Guru, Arjun Dev.

The Sikh marriage ceremony commences with the recitation of the *lavaan* hymns with the couple circumambulating *Guru Granth Sahib* clockwise. The *granthi* reads a *lav* from *Guru Granth Sahib* and the couple circumambulates the Holy Scripture with the *ragi jatha* repeating each *lav* set to music. The four *lavaan* being over, the *granthi* reads the *bani* called *Anand*. Hence, this form of marriage came to be popularly called *Anand Karaj*, which means an act of joy or bliss. The ceremony has both literal and symbolic meaning. Literally, it is a union of two individuals who, after marriage, share one light illuminating two bodies. Symbolically, it is a union of the microcosmic self with the Macrocosmic Reality. In Sikh tradition, husband and wife are expected to develop the same spiritual wavelength after marriage to begin their new life together.

In the traditional Sikh society, relatives initially identified the bride and bridegroom. These days, besides mediation from relatives, matches are also found through matrimonial services. The practice of boys and girls themselves finding suitable matches is also quite common. In the traditional

Sikh society, search for a match for a girl started soon after she reached puberty. However, with increasing urbanization and emphasis on economic independence of women, most marriages take place after brides have finished their education or, in some cases, have settled down in good jobs.

Although in theory Sikhism does not believe in caste system, in practice most marriages are arranged within the defined caste hierarchy. While parents and family elders have a major say in negotiating a marriage, boys and girls are consulted before a proposal is finalised. After verification of particulars and other related inquiries through common friends and relatives, parents of the prospective bride and groom also consult their extended families before publicly announcing the alliance.

Marriage Preparations

The first step in the marriage process is called *roka* or *kurmai*. After an alliance is decided between two families, the elders of the two families, along with the prospective bride and groom, meet either in a *gurdwara* or in the boy's residence. A *granthi* or a family elder reads the *ardaas* where he thanks the Lord for bringing two families closer and seeks His blessings for smooth completion of the marriage process. After *ardaas*, sweets are distributed among those present and the boy and girl are gifted some money. The ceremony is simple and is generally restricted to the parents. In some cases, close relatives of the boy and girl are also invited. This ritual formalizes the alliance desired by the two families and, unless there are exceptional circumstances, it is improper for either side to break the alliance. Since the Sikhs do not believe in auspicious days or months, engagement can be fixed on any mutually convenient day.

After the engagement, parents of the boy and girl meet again and a suitable date for marriage is negotiated. In fixing the marriage date several factors play their part. These include ensuring participation from the entire family, examination of children in the family so that their studies are not disrupted, prevailing weather conditions at the time, location of the two families, feasible place for the reception of the *barat* and locating a *gurdwara* in the nearby area. Further, the date is spaced so

Facing page: Wedding is a festive occasion in the family

Below: Roka *is a simple ceremony which is performed in the presence of* Guru Granth Sahib.

that both the families get sufficient time to make arrangements. Generally, two or three nearer dates are proposed and the most suitable of these is selected after discussions between the families of the bride and the groom and is announced.

From then on, marriage preparations start in right earnest and responsibilities are distributed within the family. The two families suddenly find themselves in thick of activities. Invitation cards are drawn and redrawn and the most accepted card is given to the printer. Sometimes, families try to be more innovative and thoughts are put into preparing cards for inviting people. At other times, families visit a printer and select a card on his shop, which is then given for printing. A great care is taken to finalize the language used for inviting people. Generally, parents of the boy and girl visit their relatives and friends a few days before marriage and invite them for the marriage. On this occasion, sweets are also gifted with a card for invitation.

While parents distribute cards, other members of the family perform their respective duties. A caterer is selected after a survey of the market and is booked for preparing food and sweets. Similarly, a suitable place is selected for the reception of the *barat*, according to the financial status of the family. In certain cases, *barat* is received in a lavishly decorated marriage hall or a hotel. In other cases, *barat* is received near one's residence in a specially erected tent. For these arrangements, a lot of efforts are put to find the best within one's budget.

New clothes are purchased for the bride, groom, family and relatives. A list is prepared to include relatives and friends with whom the family has *vartana* (reciprocity) relationships. A great care is taken to ensure that no one close to the family is left out. For every individual included in the list, clothes are purchased which are gifted to him/her after the marriage. Clothes are also purchased for the prospective bride and the boy's side gifts *doli* suit to the girl, which she wears before leaving her parent's home. Similarly, clothes are bought or made for all members of the family. People prepare separate clothes for all occasions during the marriage. Jewellery is bought for the bride and women of the family also engage in buying latest designs to wear in the marriage.

Facing page: Ladies of the family listening to the kirtan *during Anand Karaj*

Ring Ceremony

Ring ceremony is organised sometimes before the marriage depending upon the convenience of the two families. It is comparatively a simple affair and includes parents, some family elders and select relatives. The girl's side makes arrangement for the ceremony either at its residence or in a hotel. Boy's side is invited to the selected place. In this ceremony, the boy and girl exchange rings. Although ring ceremony is not a part of the prescribed Sikh marriage code in practice this has become an integral part of the marriage process. After the couple exchange rings, the relatives and friends present on the occasion make gifts to the boy and girl. Sweets are gifted to the boy's relatives and friends by the girl's parents and lunch is served.

Below: Ring ceremony

Shagun

A day before marriage, *shagun* ceremony is organised. By that time, almost all relatives arrive at the boy's residence. An uninterrupted recitation of *Guru Granth Sahib,* called *akhand paath,* commences at the boy's house two days before the *shagun* ceremony. On the day of *shagun* the recitation is completed. Before performing the *ardaas, a ragi jatha* sings hymns from the *Guru Granth Sahib*. The boy's side waits for the arrival of the girl's parents, brothers and close relatives. On arrival, they are received at the gate and are escorted inside. Everyone, after paying respect to the *Guru Granth Sahib,* joins the congregation and participates in the final prayer. After prayer, the *granthi* takes the *hukamnama* (Divine Order) from *Guru Granth Sahib* by

Below: Bride's parents and relatives carrying shagun

Following double spread: The groom being offered sweets during shagun

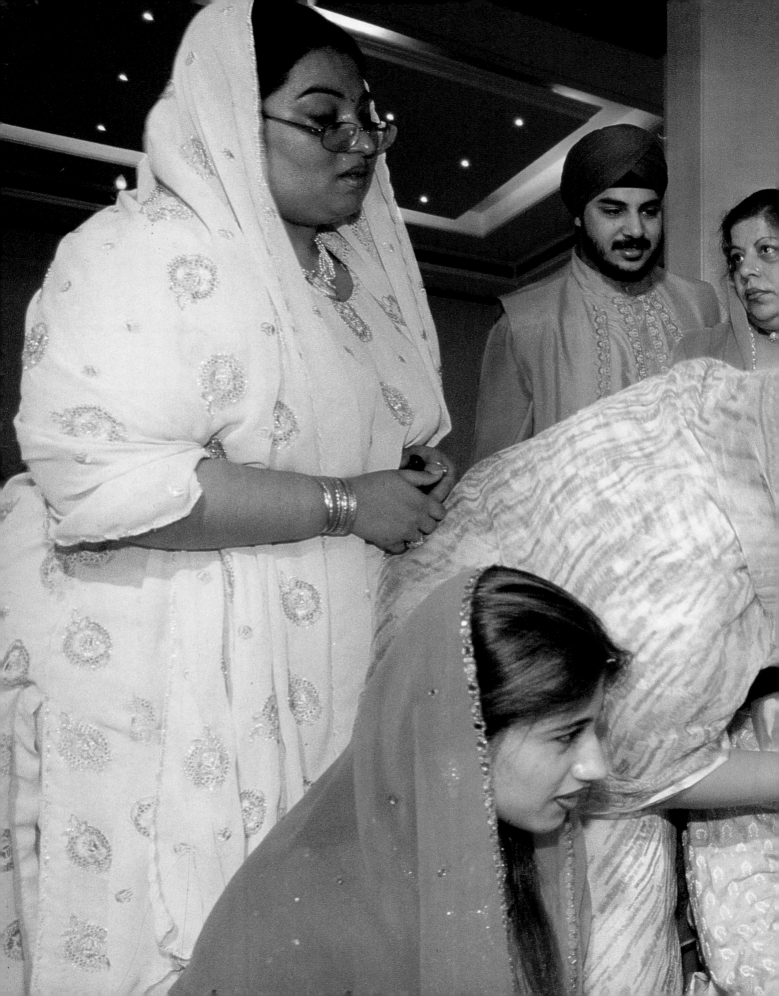

randomly opening a page and *karah prasad* (sacramental food) is distributed to the congregation.

The *granthi* then invites the girl's parents to initiate the ceremony. The girl's father puts a vermilion mark on the boy's forehead and gifts him a bracelet, a wristwatch and cash. The girl's mother, brothers and close relatives also offer cash and gifts to the boy and his relatives. After the ceremony, the boy's side serves lunch to everyone present. This is also an occasion when the boy's side invites friends and neighbours whom they are unable to include in the marriage procession to keep the *barat* within the required size.

In the evening, boy's sisters visit the girl's residence and gift her the *doli* suit and *mehndi* (henna), along with some

Girl's father putting tikka *on the boy's forehead during* shagun

jewellery. At the groom's house, the festive mood intensifies with women singing wedding songs. At the bride's house, women and girls apply *mehndi* on their hands.

At night before the departure of the *barat*, women of the family organise a night procession of light called *jago*. The procession is led by the eldest *mami* (maternal aunt) of the boy who carries a pitcher full of water on her head. This pitcher has lamps made of flour (*diyas*) placed on it. These lamps are filled with mustard oil and cotton wicks dipped in the oil are lighted. The *mami* leads the procession of women that include the boy's sisters, cousins and *bhabhis* (sisters-in-law), besides other members of the family. The group dances and sings songs, teases and entertains people in the neighbourhood through songs and dance.

Turmeric paste is applied to the body of the bride and groom before giving them a bath on the day of marriage. Amid ceremonies, they wear new clothes and get ready for the marriage. The girl's *mama* (maternal uncle) gifts her a *chura* (ivory bangles). At the boy's house, his sisters put a *sehra*

Below:
Family members and guests being applied mehndi

(right) Mehndi patterns on bride's hands

Following double spread: Jago *is taken out a day before the departure of the* barat

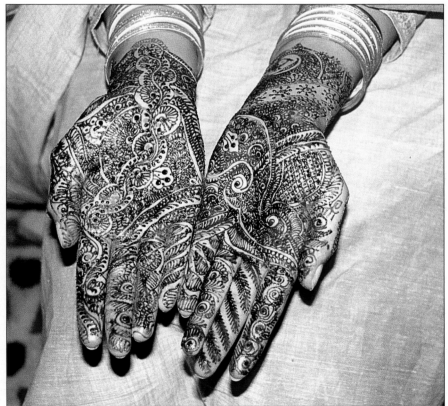

Below: Ladies singing wedding songs before the marriage. Courtesy: Sabharwal Studio

Facing page:
(Top) Mama *helping the bride wear* Chura

(Bottom) The bride decked up wearing bridal suit and chura

Following double spread: Before leaving for barat, vatna *is applied to the groom under a red* salu *carried by close relatives and sisters*

Double spread pages 34-35 and Page 36: Marriage is an occasion for joy and fun for young and old alike

Pages 37: Groom is offered sweets by his sisters

Double spread pages 38-39: Groom and his sarbala *getting ready for the marriage procession*

(chaplet) over his turban and his *bhabhi* puts *surma* (collyrium powder) in his eyes. The groom is flanked by his friends and *sarbala* (generally a younger brother who acts as an escort) and awaits the arrival of the band and mare. In case the marriage place is at a distance from the groom's residence, *baratis* travel to a nearest spot where a band and mare have already been arranged. The groom gets out of the vehicle and mounts the mare, in which his brothers and friends help him. His *sarbala* also mounts the mare. Relatives and friends dance to the tunes of latest songs in front of the mare while the groom's sisters feed the mare with pulses. The procession moves slowly as people demand it to stop after every few minutes while they dance.

31

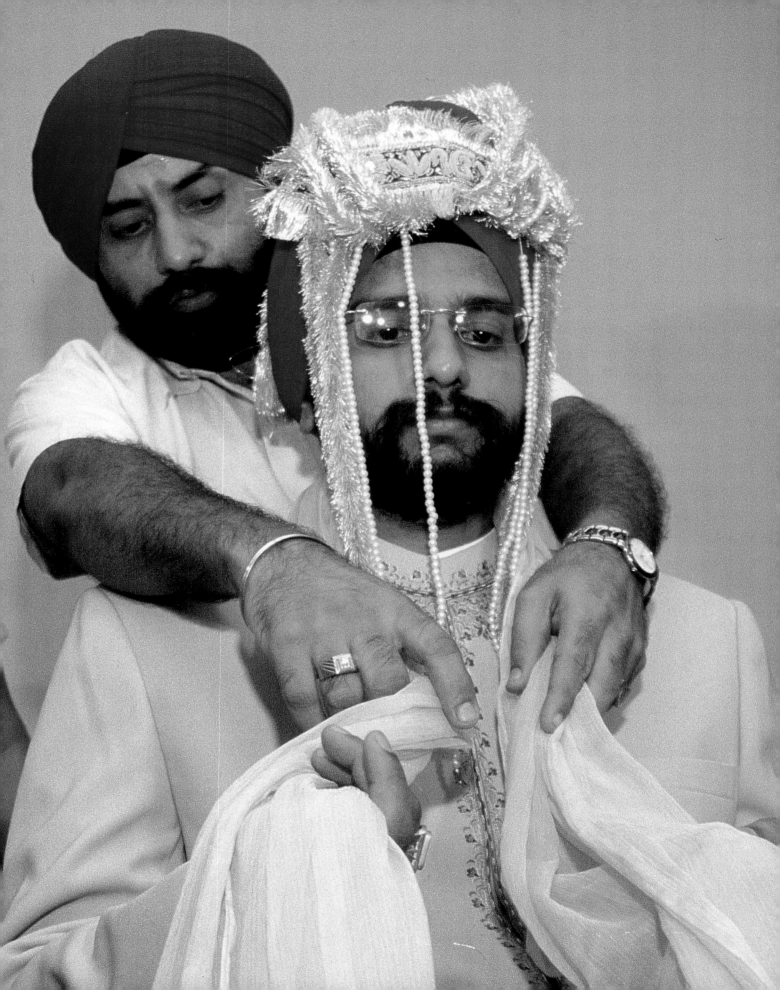

Previous double spread: Ardaas *is offered before the* barat *starts*

Left: The groom before mounting the mare

Below: The groom performs jand katna *(testing the sword)*

Facing page: Groom's sisters tie thread to the mare

Arrival of Barat and Milni

On arrival of the marriage party at the bride's place the following, hymn from *Guru Granth Sahib* is sung by the parents and other relatives of the bride:

Raag Soohee Mahalaa 1 Chhant Ghar 2
Ik Onkaar satgur prasaad.
Ham ghar saajan aae.
Saachai mel milaae.
Sahaj milaae har man bhaae panch mile sukh paa-i-aa.
Saaee wasat paraapat hoee jis setee man laa-i-aa.
Andin mel bha-i-aa man maaniaa ghar mandar sohaae.
Panch sabad dhun anhad waaje ham ghar saajan aae.1.

Measure Suhi First Guru Chhant Ghar 2

[The Creator of all is One, the only One. He is realized by the True Guru's grace. Friends have come into my home. The True Lord has brought about this union. When it pleased the Lord's

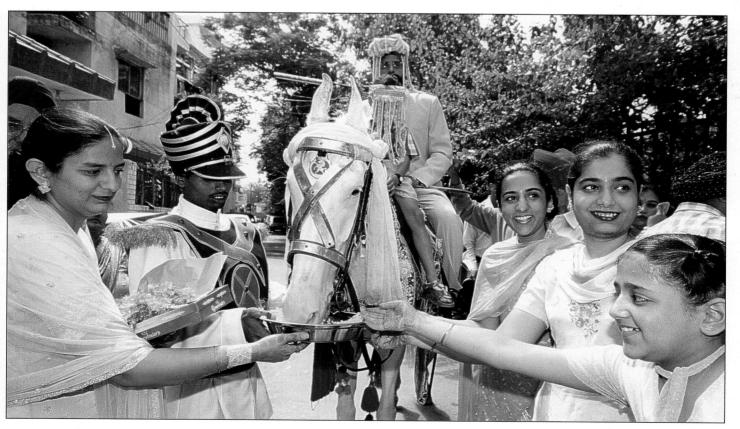

45

mind, He spontaneously caused me to meet them. By meeting the chosen ones of God, I found peace. I have obtained the very thing with which I had attached my mind. By meeting the holy in devotion, day and night my mind remains pleased and beauteous look my home and mansion. The unbeaten melodious music of the five musical instruments resounds as the loved friends have come into my home.1.]

(*Guru Granth Sahib, p.764*)

The groom's party responds by singing the following hymn:

Raag Suhi Mahalaa 1 Ghar 3
Ik Onkaar satgur prasaad.
Aavho sajnaa hao dekhaa darsan teraa raam.
Ghar aapnarai kharee takaa mai man chao ghaneraa raam.
Man chaao ghaneraa sun prabh meraa mai teraa bharvaasaa.

Below: Groom is received and blessed by bride's relatives

Darsan dekh bhaee nihkeval janam maran dukh naasaa.
Saglee jot jaataa too soee miliaa bhaae subhaae.
Nanak saajan kao bal jaaeeai saach mile ghar aae.1.

(Guru Granth Sahib, pp.764-5)

Measure Suhi First Guru Ghar 3
[The Creator of all is One, the only One. He is realized by True Guru's grace. Come, O friend, so that I may behold Thy sight. Standing at my home, I am watching for Thee. Within my mind is great yearning, O Lord, In my mind is great yearning, listen to me, O my Lord, I have faith in Thee. On seeing Thy sight I have become desireless and my pain of birth and death has fled. Amongst all is Thy light. From that light art Thou known. Through love Thou art easily met. Nanak says, I am a sacrifice unto my Friend. To the True Ones, He comes home to meet. 1.]

Below: Bride's sisters and friends blocking entrance of the groom with a rope made of flowers

49

After reciting the above hymns, *ardaas* is offered. According to popular practice, the bride's brother helps the groom get down from the mare. While the groom, his *sarbala* and friends wait, his father and other male members are received by the father and other male relatives of the bride. First, bride's father and groom's father embrace each other after mutual garlanding. The bride's relatives offer cash to the groom's father and other relatives during this ceremony called *milni*. After *milni*, *baratis* are invited for refreshments. The bride's sisters and cousins try to block the entrance of the groom and his *sarbala* through a rope made of flowers. After some bargaining in which the boy negotiates his entry by offering cash and gifts to the girl's sisters, he is also allowed to join other *baratis* for refreshment before *Anand Karaj*.

Below: Breakfast being served to the baratis *before* Anand Karaj

Facing page: Groom escorted by sarbala *is seated before* Guru Granth Sahib *before the bride joins him*

Following page: Sehra *is removed before start of* Anand Karaj

Page 53: Sehra *is given to family elders*

Double spread pages 54-55: Ardaas *is offered before initiating* Anand Karaj

Double spread pages 56-57: Bride's father hands over palla *to the groom before initiating* Anand Karaj

Anand Karaj

According to prescribed Sikh code of conduct, the *Anand Karaj* is supposed to be performed during a simple ceremony in the ambrosial hours after *kirtan* of *Asa di Var*. But in actual practice, generally *Anand Karaj* ceremonies are performed a little before lunch time. The place where *Guru Granth Sahib* is placed is cleaned, carpets are placed on the floor, a clean bedsheet spread and *chandoa* (canopy) fixed before installation of the Holy Book. Thereupon members from both sides sit in the especially decorated place. The groom and the bride are then made to sit before *Guru Granth Sahib*.

Thereafter, the *granthi* announces the names of the boy and the girl and asks their parents to reaffirm their consent for the marriage. The *granthi* then asks the fathers of the bride and

Below: Anand Karaj of baptised couples being performed during ambrosial hours in a simple ceremony as per Sikh maryada

Facing page: The groom and the bride sit before Guru Granth Sahib.

Following double spread: The couple circumambulates Guru Granth Sahib

Double spread pages 64-65: After the completion of every lav, *the couple bows before* Guru Granth Sahib

the bridegroom to stand up and offer prayer invoking the Lord's blessings to start the *Anand Karaj* while the rest of the congregation keeps sitting. Before the start of the *lavaan*, the *granthi* normally advises the bride and the groom, explaining the spiritual significance of the married life in which they are going to enter.

The priest also advises the couple to get baptised in case they have not already done so. The *granthi* then calls upon the father of the bride to pass over the hem of a scarf to the groom symbolically conveying the message that the girl, who had so far enjoyed the protection of her father, henceforth shall come under the protection of her husband. This ceremony is called *palla pharana*. The *ragis* then sing the following hymn:

Salok M: 5.
Ustat nindaa Nanak jee mai habh wanjaaee
Chhoriaa habh kijh tiaagee.
Habhe saak kooraave dithe tao palai taidai laagee.1.
(Guru Granth Sahib, p. 963)

Slok Fifth Guru.
[O reverend Nanak, I have wholly discarded praising and slandering others hand have forsaken, renounced all other worldly affairs. I have found all other relationships to be false. I have attached myself to Thy lappet, O Lord.1.]

The *granthi* then reads from the *Guru Granth Sahib* the hymns of *lavaan* composed by Guru Ram Das. The verses are first read from *Guru Granth Sahib* while the couple is sitting in front. The same *lav* is repeated through singing by the *ragis* with the couple circumambulating *Guru Granth Sahib* in the clockwise direction. The groom walks ahead and is followed by the bride. The couple tries to synchronise the circle with the singing of each *lav*. After the completion of each circle, the couple bows before the *Guru Granth Sahib* and sits until the next verse is read. This is performed four times, each time the *granthi* reciting one *lav* from the *Guru Granth Sahib* and the *ragis* repeating the same *lav* set to music (For text of the four *lavaan* see Appendix I). On the completion of the fourth and the last

Facing page: The newly wed couple is offered advice by the Sikh priest

Following double spread: Priest offers prayer on the successful completion of Anand ceremony

lav flower petals are showered upon the couple by relatives and friends though this practice is generally discouraged by the *granthi*. Before recitation of the *Anand* the following hymn is generally sung by the *ragis*:

Siri Raag Mahalaa 4 Ghar 2 Chhant

Veeaah hoaa mere baabulaa gurmukhe har paa-i-aa.
Agiaan andheraa katiaa gur giaan parchand balaa-i-aa.
Baliaa gurgiaan anderaa binsiaa har ratan padaarath laadhaa.
Haomai rog ga-i-aa dukh laathaa aap aapai gurmat khaadhaa.
Akaal moorat var paa-i-aa abinaasee naa kade marai
na jaa-i-aa.
Veeaah hoaa mere baabolaa gurmukhe har paa-i-aa. 2.

(*Guru Granth Sahib, p. 78*)

Measure Fourth Guru Ghar 2 Chhant (lyrics)
My marriage is performed, O my father. By Guru's guidance, I have obtained God. The darkness of my ignorance is removed. The Guru has blazed a very bright light of Divine knowledge in me. The Guru-given Divine knowledge is giving lustre and the darkness has gone. I have found the priceless gem of God's Name. My malady of ego has gone and my troubles are over. With Guru's guidance, I, myself, have eaten my self-conceit. I have procured God of immortal form as my Spouse. He is imperishable so does not die or go. O my father, my marriage has been solemnised and by Guru's guidance, I have found God. 2.

Hukumnama *is taken from* Guru Granth Sahib *after* ardaas

The ritual concludes with the singing of the first five and the last stanzas of the *Anand* followed by *ardaas*. The *hukum* or *wak* (the Divine Command) is then taken by the *granthi* from the *Guru Granth Sahib* by opening it at random. Thereafter, the congregation is served with *karah prasad* (sacramental food) with which the ceremony concludes. Both sides then felicitate each other and offer garlands and *shagun* to the newly married couple and pose for photographs. Sometimes, a male child is put in the lap of the bride giving her a subtle hint to raise family soon after marriage and hoping she will bear a male child. Bride's

Below: The couple being garlanded by the granthi after the Anand ceremony

Following double spread: Parents and relatives blessing the newly wed couple

sister and younger brothers hide the shoes of the groom when the marriage ceremony is going on. The shoes are returned to the groom after negotiations where he offers some gifts to the younger relatives of the bride.

Below: The couple being garlanded by the granthi *after the Anand ceremony*

Following double spread: Parents and relatives blessing the newly wed couple

Facing page: Newly wed couple

Right:
(Top) Family elders blessing the newly weds

(Bottom) Women greeting each other after the wedding

Following page:
(Top) Barati *helping themselves with lunch*

(Bottom) Bride's relatives carrying the shagun *offerings*

Page 75: Bride's sisters and younger brothers negotiate with the groom to return his shoes

Double spread pages 76-77: A young male child is put in the lap of the bride suggesting her to start the family soon

Double spread pages 78-79: Ardaas is offered before departure of the doli

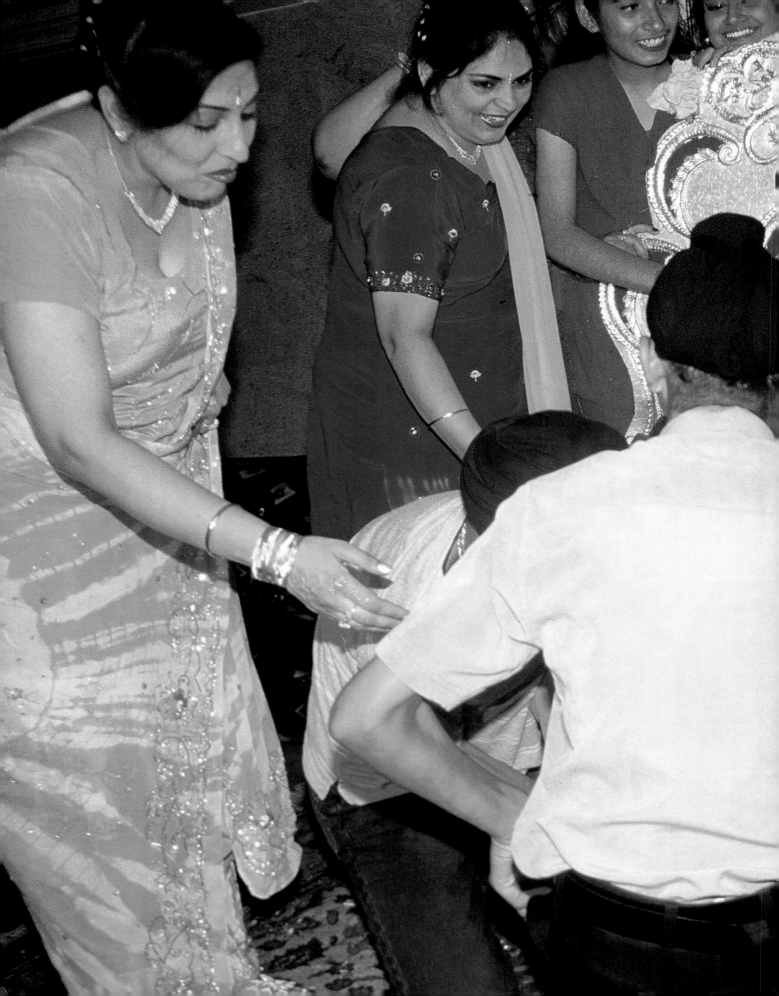

Doli

After *lavaan*, the bride and groom are escorted back to the marriage venue in case the ceremony is performed in a place different from the place where the marriage party is staying. Relatives and friends from both sides present gifts to the newly wed couple, and bless them for a happy married life. Simultaneously, lunch is served to the *barat* and the couple is brought to one of the tables. Sisters, mother and father of the groom flank the couple and they sit together and eat. This symbolizes that the bride is now a part of the family by virtue of sharing the meal together. The atmosphere remains one of fun and frolic. During this time, the bride's mother presents gifts to the groom's mother and other female relatives, which is considered a part of the *milni* performed earlier on the arrival of the *barat* where only males participate in the ceremony.

Below: The bride throwing puffed rice over her head wishing prosperity for the house she leaves

Facing page: Specially decorated doli *(wooden palanquin) is seldom seen these days*

Following double spread: Bride is carried to the doli *by her relatives*

Double spread pages 84-85: Decorated luxury cars have replaced traditional doli

Double spread pages 86-87: Departure of the doli

While the groom sits with his friends, the bride retires to the adjoining room and changes her dress. Now she wears the specially prepared *doli* dress given to her by the groom's family. During this time music or band is played to entertain the *baratis* as they await the arrival of the bride. After some time, the bride arrives escorted by her sisters and sisters-in-law and sits with the groom. Generally, the *doli* leaves before it gets dark. The newly wed couple, their parents and some other relatives assemble and *ardaas* is offered again. This need not be performed in a gurdwara or by a *granthi*. In fact, any elder member of either family can offer the *ardaas* where the families thank God for His grace at the successful conclusion of the entire ceremony and seek His blessings for the newly weds. Before leaving her parental home, the bride throws pulses or rice over her head wishing prosperity for the parental home she is leaving.

The brother of the bride and other relatives escort her to the *doli* (palanquin). These days cars decorated with flowers are used in place of the traditional *doli* carried by *kahars* (professional palanquin bearers). After the bride gets into the car, the groom's father throws coins over the *doli* as a symbol of prosperity this alliance will bring to the family. The bride leaves amidst singing of traditional songs wherein young girls create an emotionally surcharged atmosphere through various similes contained in the songs, indicating helplessness of the father who is unable to keep his daughter home any longer.

Bride in her New Home

Upon arrival at the home of the groom, his mother welcomes the newly wed couple in the house. She puts some oil at the *choukhat* (opposite ends of the door). This ceremony is called *tel chauna*. The boy's mother receives the newly wed couple at the gate of the house with a bowl filled with water which she moves over the head of the couple seven times and drinks a small quantity of water each time. The seventh time everyone tries to stop her. This symbolizes the willingness of the boy's mother to take upon her all future troubles of the couple. This ritual is called *pani varna*. The bride is then taken round the house and is brought to the place where all the relatives have assembled. There the relatives of the boy offer cash and gifts to the bride. This ceremony is called *muhn dikhai* or *ghund chukai* (unveiling of bride). Although they all have seen the bride before and during the marriage, the ceremony continues to be performed as part of the traditional ritual.

To help the bride feel at home in the new environs the couple is asked to engage in certain games. A *parat* (deep plate) is filled with milk mixed with water and a coin is thrown in it. The couple is expected to find the coin. It is believed that whosoever finds the coin first becomes dominant in the new relationship. In spite of emphasis on gender equality, it is expected of the bride that she should pretend not being able to find the coin and accept the upper hand of the groom in this game.

The bride is received after the ceremony of pani varna

Above: A newly wed couple at the Golden Temple

Facing page: A bride preparing her first meal in her in-laws' home

Another game called *gune khedna* is played where an elder woman in the family puts *ladoos* (sweets) in the palm of the groom, which are caught by the bride when the groom loosens his grip. These are put back in the palm of the groom. This exercise is repeated a few times by the bride with the groom and later with her mother-in-law and other relatives. Thereafter *ladoos* are distributed among the guests. Then *gand kholna* is played wherein the bride tries to open the thread tied on the wrist of the groom a day before marriage by his sisters and sister-in-law. The bride is expected to open the knot successfully. Ceremonies being over, the relatives and friends leave and the couple consummate their marriage.

The next morning the bride and the groom, along with the groom's parents, generally visit a local gurdwara thanking the Almighty for the alliance and seeking blessings for the days to come. On the same day, the couple visits the bride's house, which is called *fera pana*, where they have lunch. If parents of the girl are in the same city, the couple returns in the evening. Another ritual called *chauke charna* (entering the kitchen) is performed where the bride is asked to prepare the first meal in her in-laws' house and serve it to everyone in the family. She is offered some cash by her mother-in-law by way of *shagun*. While various social customs before and after the marriage differ from one caste group to another, *Anand Karaj* continues to be the normative marriage practice among the Sikhs in India and abroad.

ਸੂਹੀ ਮਹਲਾ ੪ ॥

ਹਰਿ ਪਹਿਲੜੀ ਲਾਵ ਪਰਵਿਰਤੀ ਕਰਮ ਦ੍ਰਿੜਾਇਆ ਬਲਿ ਰਾਮ ਜੀਉ ॥
ਬਾਣੀ ਬ੍ਰਹਮਾ ਵੇਦੁ ਧਰਮੁ ਦ੍ਰਿੜਹੁ ਪਾਪ ਤਜਾਇਆ ਬਲਿ ਰਾਮ ਜੀਉ ॥
ਧਰਮੁ ਦ੍ਰਿੜਹੁ ਹਰਿ ਨਾਮੁ ਧਿਆਵਹੁ ਸਿਮ੍ਰਿਤਿ ਨਾਮੁ ਦ੍ਰਿੜਾਇਆ ॥
ਸਤਿਗੁਰੁ ਗੁਰੁ ਪੂਰਾ ਆਰਾਧਹੁ ਸਭਿ ਕਿਲਵਿਖ ਪਾਪ ਗਵਾਇਆ ॥
ਸਹਜ ਅਨੰਦੁ ਹੋਆ ਵਡਭਾਗੀ ਮਨਿ ਹਰਿ ਹਰਿ ਮੀਠਾ ਲਾਇਆ ॥
ਜਨੁ ਕਹੈ ਨਾਨਕੁ ਲਾਵ ਪਹਿਲੀ ਆਰੰਭੁ ਕਾਜੁ ਰਚਾਇਆ ॥ ੧ ॥

ਹਰਿ ਦੂਜੜੀ ਲਾਵ ਸਤਿਗੁਰੁ ਪੁਰਖੁ ਮਿਲਾਇਆ ਬਲਿ ਰਾਮ ਜੀਉ ॥
ਨਿਰਭਉ ਭੈ ਮਨੁ ਹੋਇ ਹਉਮੈ ਮੈਲੁ ਗਵਾਇਆ ਬਲਿ ਰਾਮ ਜੀਉ ॥
ਨਿਰਮਲੁ ਭਉ ਪਾਇਆ ਹਰਿ ਗੁਣ ਗਾਇਆ ਹਰਿ ਵੇਖੈ ਰਾਮੁ ਹਦੂਰੇ ॥
ਹਰਿ ਆਤਮ ਰਾਮੁ ਪਸਾਰਿਆ ਸੁਆਮੀ ਸਰਬ ਰਹਿਆ ਭਰਪੂਰੇ ॥
ਅੰਤਰਿ ਬਾਹਰਿ ਹਰਿ ਪ੍ਰਭੁ ਏਕੋ ਮਿਲਿ ਹਰਿ ਜਨ ਮੰਗਲ ਗਾਏ ॥
ਜਨ ਨਾਨਕ ਦੂਜੀ ਲਾਵ ਚਲਾਈ ਅਨਹਦ ਸਬਦ ਵਜਾਏ ॥ ੨ ॥

ਹਰਿ ਤੀਜੜੀ ਲਾਵ ਮਨਿ ਚਾਉ ਭਇਆ ਬੈਰਾਗੀਆ ਬਲਿ ਰਾਮ ਜੀਉ ॥
ਸੰਤ ਜਨਾ ਹਰਿ ਮੇਲੁ ਹਰਿ ਪਾਇਆ ਵਡਭਾਗੀਆ ਬਲਿ ਰਾਮ ਜੀਉ ॥
ਨਿਰਮਲੁ ਹਰਿ ਪਾਇਆ ਹਰਿ ਗੁਣ ਗਾਇਆ ਮੁਖਿ ਬੋਲੀ ਹਰਿ ਬਾਣੀ ॥
ਸੰਤ ਜਨਾ ਵਡਭਾਗੀ ਪਾਇਆ ਹਰਿ ਕਥੀਐ ਅਕਥ ਕਹਾਣੀ ॥
ਹਿਰਦੈ ਹਰਿ ਹਰਿ ਹਰਿ ਧੁਨਿ ਉਪਜੀ ਹਰਿ ਜਪੀਐ ਮਸਤਕਿ ਭਾਗੁ ਜੀਉ ॥
ਜਨੁ ਨਾਨਕੁ ਬੋਲੇ ਤੀਜੀ ਲਾਵੈ ਹਰਿ ਉਪਜੈ ਮਨਿ ਬੈਰਾਗੁ ਜੀਉ ॥ ੩ ॥

ਹਰਿ ਚਉਥੜੀ ਲਾਵ ਮਨਿ ਸਹਜੁ ਭਇਆ ਹਰਿ ਪਾਇਆ ਬਲਿ ਰਾਮ ਜੀਉ॥
ਗੁਰਮੁਖਿ ਮਿਲਿਆ ਸੁਭਾਇ ਹਰਿ ਮਨਿ ਤਨਿ ਮੀਠਾ ਲਾਇਆ ਬਲਿ ਰਾਮ ਜੀਉ॥
ਹਰਿ ਮੀਠਾ ਲਾਇਆ ਮੇਰੇ ਪ੍ਰਭ ਭਾਇਆ ਅਨਦਿਨੁ ਹਰਿ ਲਿਵ ਲਾਈ ॥
ਮਨ ਚਿੰਦਿਆ ਫਲੁ ਪਾਇਆ ਸੁਆਮੀ ਹਰਿ ਨਾਮਿ ਵਜੀ ਵਾਧਾਈ ॥
ਹਰਿ ਪ੍ਰਭਿ ਠਾਕੁਰਿ ਕਾਜੁ ਰਚਾਇਆ ਧਨ ਹਿਰਦੈ ਨਾਮਿ ਵਿਗਾਸੀ ॥
ਜਨੁ ਨਾਨਕੁ ਬੋਲੇ ਚਉਥੀ ਲਾਵੈ ਹਰਿ ਪਾਇਆ ਪ੍ਰਭੁ ਅਵਿਨਾਸੀ ॥ ੪ ॥ ੨ ॥

(ਸ੍ਰੀ ਗੁਰੂ ਗ੍ਰੰਥ ਸਾਹਿਬ, ਪੰਨਾ ੭੭੩-੭੭੪)

SUHI MAHALAA 4.

Har pahilaree laav parvirtee karam driraa-i-aa baliraam jeeo. Baanee brahmaa ved dharam drirho paap tajaa-i-aa baliraam jeeo. Dharam drirho harinaam dhiaavho simrit naam driraa-i-aa. Satguru guru pooraa aaraadhho sabh kilvikh paap gavaa-i-aa. Sahaj anand hoaa wadbhaagee man har har meethaa laa-i-aa. Jan kahai Nanak laav pahlee aarambh kaaj rachaa-i-aa. 1.

Har doojaree laav satguru purakh milaa-i-aa baliraam jeeo. Nirbhao bhai man hoe haomai mail gavaa-i-aa baliraam jeeo. Nirmal bhao paa-i-aa har gun gaa-i-aa har vekhai raam hadoore. Har aatamraam pasaariaa suaamee sarab rahiaa bharpoore. Antar baahar harprabh eko mil har jan mangal gaae. Jan Nanak doojee laav chalaaee anhad sabad vajaae.2.

Har teejaree laav man chaao bha-i-aa bairaageeaa baliraam jeeo. Sant janaa har mel har paa-i-aa wadbhaageeaa baliraam jeeo. Nirmal har paa-i-aa har gun gaa-i-aa mukh bolee har baanee. Sant janaa wadhbhaagee paa-i-aa har katheeai akath kahaanee. Hirdai har har har dhun upjee har japeeai mastak bhaag jeeo. Jan Nanak bole teejee laavai har upjai man bairaag jeeo. 3.

Har chaotharee laav man sahaj bha-i-aa har paa-i-aa baliram jeeo. Gurmukh miliaa subhaae har man tan meethaa laa-i-aa baliraam jeeo. Har meethaa laa-i-aa mere prabh bhaa-i-aa andin har liv laaee. Man chindiaa phal paa-i-aa suaamee harinaam wajee waadhaaee. Hariprabh thaakur kaaj rachaa-i-aa dhan hirdai naam wigaasee. Jan Nanak bole chaothee laavai har paa-i-aa prabh avinaasee. 4.2.

SUHI MAHALAA 4.

In the first Round, the Lord instructs thee to revolve back to the world,

And to look upon the Guru's Word as the Veda, to practise Righteousness,
and so to dispel thy Sins.

Practise thou Righteousness and Dwell upon the Lord's Name-the Smiritis too inculcate
but the Lord's Name-

And Dwell upon thy Perfect Guru that all thy Sins are Eradicated.

Thy Fortune will smile, and the Bliss of Poise wilt thou gather, and the Lord will seem
Pleasing to thee.

Sayeth Nanak : "In the first Round, the Lord Himself initiates His Marriage with thee". {1}

In the second Round, thy Lord Unites thee with thy True Guru, the Cosmic Being,

And, thou becomest Fear-free, save for the Lord's Fear in thy Mind, and thou art rid of
the Dirt of I-amness.

Thy Fear, now, is of thy Immaculate Lord, and, Singing the Lord's Praise, thou See-est
His Presence.

And thou See-est the All-pervading, All-filling Lord.

Thy only Lord is both within and without ; Meeting with the Saints, Sing thou the Song of
Joy.

Sayeth Nanak : "In the second Round, the Unstruck Metody of the Word Ringeth in thy
Mind". {2}

In the third Round, the Joy of Detachment wells up in thy mind.

Meeting with the Saints, thou Meetest thy Lord and Fortune smiles on thee.

Thou Attainest thy Immaculate God and Singest His Praise and thou utterest the Lord's
Word with thy tongue.

Thou Attainest to the Lord, O Saintly being, and Utterest the Truth that is unutterable.

In thy Mind Ringeth the Music of the Lord, and thou Contemplatest Him, for thy Lot now
shines forth.

Sayeth Nanak : "In the third Round, Divine Detachedness wells up in thy Mind". {3}

In the fourth Round, thy Mind is held in Poise, for thou hast Attained to thy Lord.

All-too-spontaneously hath thy Lord Met thee, by the Guru's Grace, and thy God seemeth
Sweet to thee.

Seemeth Sweet to thee thy God, who Loveth thee, and thou art ever Attuned to Him.

And thou Attainest thy heart's Desire, thy Lord, thy God ; and the Glory of the Lord's
Name Ringeth in thy Mind.

Thy Master hath brought about thy Wedding with Him and thy heart, O Bride, is in
Bloom, being Illumined by the Name.

Sayeth Nanak : "In the fourth Round, thou Attainest to thy Eternal Lord". {4}

(*Sri Guru Granth Sahib*, English Translation Dr. Gopal Singh, Vol III, p.736)

Top: A Janamsakhi *painting depicting Guru Nanak's marriage procession.*

Right: Departure of Doli

Courtsey: Prof. Pritam Singh

Glossary

Anand Karaj	Literally, a joyous act. In common parlance it is used for Sikh form of marriage
Ardaas	Sikh prayer
Barat	Marriage party
Bhabi	Brother's wife
Chakki	Grindstone
Chandoa	Canopy
Dharmshala	Rest house
Dohri dastar	Turban tied after covering the head with a scarf
Doli	A decorated palanquin used for carrying the bride
Garwi	A small pitcher
Ghund chukai/muhn dikhai	Ceremonial unveiling of the bride
Gotra	The sub-group in a caste
Granthi	Professional reader of Sikh scriptures
Gur	Jaggery
Gursikh	Pious Sikh
Jago	A procession with lights carried out a night before marriage
Kahar	Palanquin bearers
Kesar	Saffron colour
Khande da Pahul	Baptismal nectar prepared through double-edged sword
Kirpan	Small sword, one of the five Sikh symbols
Kurmai	Engagement
Lassi	A drink made of mixing curd and water
Lavaan	Circumambulation of the *Guru Granth Sahib*
Maaiaan	A period of seclusion before marriage
Mahurat	Auspicious time
Mami	Maternal uncle's wife
Mangna	Engagement
Maryada	Convention
Mela	Festival
Milni	Ceremonial meeting between the close relatives from the bride's and groom's side
Misl	A term which originated in the eighteenth-century history of the Sikhs to describe a unit or brigade of Sikh warriors and the record of territories acquired by them. In late eighteenth century there were twelve important *misls*
Mukut	A kind of headgear
Nionda	Offering meal to family members and friends
Panchayat	Assembly of respected village elders
Pani varna	A ritual performed by the groom's mother
Parda	Veil
Parat	Large, deep plate
Ragi jatha	Sikh hymn singers
Sahe di chitthi	Letter fixing marriage date
Saha kadhna	To find the auspicious date of marriage
Sarika	Collaterals
Sarbala	Groom's escort
Shabad	Hymn
Shagan	Gifts offered to the bride or groom
Sehra	Chaplet
Surma	Collyrium powder applied in eyes
Thaka	Engagement
Vartana sambandh	Relationships of exchange between relatives
Wazir	Minister